The Little Lost Lamb

Written and Illustrated by Geri Berger Haines

Pauline
BOOKS & MEDIA
Boston

Library of Congress Cataloging-in-Publication Data

Haines, Geri Berger.
  The little lost lamb / written and illustrated by Geri Berger Haines.
     p. cm.
   ISBN 0-8198-4528-0
   1. Lost sheep (Parable)--Juvenile literature. I. Title.
   BT378.L6H35 2009
   226.8′09505--dc22
                            2008021625

"P" and PAULINE are registered trademarks of the Daughters of St. Paul.

Copyright © 2001, 2009, Daughters of St. Paul

Published by Pauline Books & Media, 50 Saint Paul's Avenue, Boston, MA 02130-3491

Printed in Korea.

LLL SIPSKOGUNKYO6-6016 4528-0

www.pauline.org

Pauline Books & Media is the publishing house of the Daughters of St. Paul, an international congregation of women religious serving the Church with the communications media.

For my two little lambs
(who have grown up to be big sheep),
that they may always follow
the footsteps of the Good Shepherd.

High on a hill, in a land far away, lived a flock of sheep. They were happy sheep.

They grazed together peacefully and enjoyed life, for they were cared for by a most kind shepherd.

This shepherd loved his sheep and would do anything for them. He fed them, tended them, and watched over them lovingly, even when they slept.

There was one lamb, though, who wasn't happy being with the flock. He just couldn't see why the flock had to stay with the shepherd.

"There must be more exciting things in life!" he thought.

One night, while everyone else was sleeping, the little lamb decided to leave the flock.

"I'll have some real fun," he told himself.

And away he trotted...

…Away from his mother…and father…
away from his sisters and brothers,
and worst of all, away from the kind
shepherd who loved him so.

"They won't care," he thought. "I'm growing up to be a big sheep like the rest of them. I can take care of myself now!"

The next morning, the little lamb was running and frolicking. He had great fun investigating different places he had never seen before.

"Wow, this is exciting!" he thought.

Finally the lamb came to a winding,
bubbling brook, where he stopped short.
Although it looked rather dangerous
to cross, he decided to try anyway.

Carefully he stepped onto some big stones. They were very slippery and… WHOOPS! In he fell!

"My leg!" he cried.

The little lamb got slowly to his feet.

"My leg!" he sobbed. "Oh, how it hurts!"

He limped over to the grass.

"Maybe I should go back home now," he thought. "But I've already come such a long way. I may as well keep going."

By now it was starting to get dark, and the little lamb was tired. He hadn't slept at all the night before, so he nestled against a tree and began to snooze…

All at once
the little lamb woke up
to a terrible sound.

CAW! CAW!

High above him were screeching buzzards—
big, ugly birds who would do anything to find
a good meal!

He quickly got up and began to run as fast as his shaky legs would take him. This new place wasn't at all what he thought it would be. He was supposed to be having fun!

"Some fun!" he thought.

He hobbled along until he spotted a cave.

"I'll be safe from those birds here," he decided.

But he had just entered the deep, dark cave when he saw…a pair of big, fierce eyes staring at him!

The little lamb shook with fright. The eyes crept slowly toward him. Now he saw not just eyes, but a set of huge, sharp teeth as well!

Out of the cave raced the little lamb, chased by a ferocious wolf!

"I wish I were home again!" he cried.

Through bushes and thickets and thorns he ran, panting and crying, until his aching leg could no longer hold him up.

Exhausted, the little lamb fell to the ground. He thought it was the end for him. He hid his eyes so he wouldn't see what was going to happen.

He had never been so afraid in all his life!
Suddenly he heard footsteps approaching.
Then he felt something softly touch his
wooly coat.

Much to the lamb's amazement, strong hands lifted him high into the air.

It was his shepherd!

"I'm so happy to see you," the little lamb cried. "I'll never run away again!"

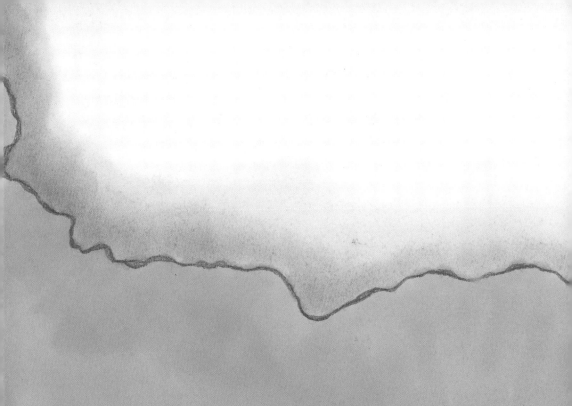

The good shepherd looked at the
lamb lovingly and cradled him in
his arms. He was so happy to find
his lost lamb that he didn't even
think about the problems the little
runaway had caused.

The gentle shepherd carried the little lamb back to his flock. There he took care of bandaging the lamb's leg. All the other sheep were already fast asleep.

The next morning, the little lamb's mother and father and sisters and brothers were so happy to see him! They crowded around him as the good shepherd watched with joy.

"What could be better than this?" the little lamb wondered.

"This is where I'm safe. This is where I'm loved!"

BOOKS & MEDIA

The Daughters of St. Paul operate book and media centers at the following addresses. Visit, call or write the one nearest you today, or find us on the World Wide Web, www.pauline.org

CALIFORNIA

3908 Sepulveda Blvd, Culver City, CA 90230	310-397-8676
935 Brewster Avenue, Redwood City, CA 94063	650-369-4230
5945 Balboa Avenue, San Diego, CA 92111	858-565-9181

FLORIDA

145 S.W. 107th Avenue, Miami, FL 33174	305-559-6715

HAWAII

1143 Bishop Street, Honolulu, HI 96813	808-521-2731
Neighbor Islands call:	866-521-2731

ILLINOIS

172 North Michigan Avenue, Chicago, IL 60601	312-346-4228

LOUISIANA

4403 Veterans Memorial Blvd, Metairie, LA 70006	504-887-7631

MASSACHUSETTS

885 Providence Hwy, Dedham, MA 02026	781-326-5385

MISSOURI

9804 Watson Road, St. Louis, MO 63126	314-965-3512

NEW YORK

64 W. 38th Street, New York, NY 10018	212-754-1110

PENNSYLVANIA

9171-A Roosevelt Blvd, Philadelphia, PA 19114	215-676-9494

SOUTH CAROLINA

243 King Street, Charleston, SC 29401	843-577-0175

VIRGINIA

1025 King Street, Alexandria, VA 22314	703-549-3806

CANADA

3022 Dufferin Street, Toronto, ON M6B 3T5	416-781-9131

¡También somos su fuente para libros, videos y música en español!